CHARLES DICKENS AND THE LAW

BY

THOMAS ALEXANDER FYFE

THE LAWBOOK EXCHANGE, LTD.
Clark, New Jersey

ISBN 978-1-58477-666-6

Lawbook Exchange edition 2006, 2020

The quality of this reprint is equivalent to the quality of the original work.

THE LAWBOOK EXCHANGE, LTD.

33 Terminal Avenue
Clark, New Jersey 07066-1321

*Please see our website for a selection of our other publications
and fine facsimile reprints of classic works of legal history:*
www.lawbookexchange.com

Library of Congress Cataloging-in-Publication Data

Fyfe, Thomas Alexander, 1853-1928.
  Charles Dickens and the law / Thomas Alexander Fyfe.
    p. cm.
  Originally published: Edinburgh : W. Hodge & Co. ; London :
Chapman and Hall, 1910.
  ISBN 1-58477-666-8 (acid-free paper)
  1. Dickens, Charles, 1812-1870—Characters—Lawyers. 2.
Dickens, Charles, 1812-1870—Knowledge—Law. 3. Lawyers
in literature. 4. Law in literature. I. Title.

PR4592.L2F94 2005
823'.8—dc22   2005004756

Printed in the United States of America on acid-free paper

CHARLES DICKENS
AND THE LAW

BY

THOMAS ALEXANDER FYFE

LONDON
CHAPMAN & HALL, LIMITED
EDINBURGH: WILLIAM HODGE & COMPANY

PRINTED BY
WILLIAM HODGE AND COMPANY
GLASGOW AND EDINBURGH
1910

PREFACE

THE following pages embody a Lecture which I recently delivered to the Glasgow Dickens Society. At the request of the Society, I have revised it for publication in book form.

T. A. F.

GLASGOW, *October*, 1910.

CHARLES DICKENS AND THE LAW

CHARLES DICKENS was pre-eminently the novelist of the law, and his lawyers have a hold upon the public imagination far surpassing that of any other author. But, although his lawyer creations are most widely known, he is not the only author who has built a tale upon a legal foundation. A few references selected at random may be interesting by way of contrast.

Next to "Bleak House" of Dickens, perhaps the most sustained literary effort of this description is that delightful, if somewhat long-drawn-out, tale of seventy years ago—nowadays, I fear, seldom read, even

by the young lawyer—"Ten Thousand a
Year," written by Samuel Warren, who was
himself a lawyer, and who built a long tale
upon a flaw in an estate title—a tale which
involved not one, but *several* lawsuits, not
less intricate than *Jarndyce and Jarndyce*, the
famous Chancery suit upon which Dickens
built his chief legal novel.   In this book
Warren created Quirk, Gamin & Snap, who
held the field as representing the type
of sharp-practice solicitor till put in the
shade by Dodson & Fogg of "Pickwick"
fame.

Anthony Trollope, in his book "Orley
Farm," produced a novel of the law which
contains some striking legal characters,
including that typical old-time barrister
Mr. Furnival, K.C., M.P., and that delightful and eccentric Old Bailey practitioner
Mr. Chaffanbrass, whose personality is akin
to more than one of the Dickens creations,

and whose portrait, as thus pen-painted by Trollope, is quite in the Dickens style :

In person Mr. Chaffanbrass is a little man, and a very dirty little man. He has all manner of nasty tricks about him, which make him a disagreeable neighbour. His wig is never at ease upon his head, but is poked by him, sometimes over one ear, and sometimes over the other, now on the back of his head, and then on his nose; and it is impossible to say in which guise he looks most cruel, most sharp, and most intolerable. His linen is never clean, his hands never washed, and his clothes never new. *But his tongue—that* moves—*there* is the weapon which he knows how to use.

Smollett had rather an ambition after legal portraiture, and in his legal novel "Sir Launcelot Greaves" he gives this full-length portrait of a young and painfully respectable attorney :

Tom Clarke was a young fellow whose goodness of heart even the exercise of his profession had not been able to corrupt. Before strangers he never owned himself an attorney without blushing, though he had no reason to blush for his own practice, for he constantly refused to engage in the cause of any client whose character was equivocal, and was never known to act with such industry as when concerned for the widow and orphan, or any other that sued *in forma pauperis*. Indeed, he was so replete with human kindness that, as often as an afflicting story or circumstance was told in his hearing, it overflowed in his eyes.

One cannot help thinking that this most exemplary young lawyer must have been amongst the good who die young. He is the type of young lawyer who could not have failed to be a bore, and we are not surprised that the portrait goes on to say :

He piqued himself on understanding the practice of the Courts, and in private company he took pleasure in laying down the law.

Perhaps human nature is perverse, but I fear this is *not* the type of lawyer the public craves to see represented on the stage or presented to them in the pages of fiction, and it is not surprising that " Sir Launcelot Greaves" was Smollett's least successful novel. His lawyers, however, were not all impossibly good like Mr. Tom Clarke. In " Ferdinand,

Count Fathom," we meet a different type of attorney. His fortune was made—as has happened before and since—by special ingenuity in the construction of bills of costs, and one cannot but sympathise with his luckless client who found that his lawyer's bill included 350 consultation fees in the course of a year of only 365 days including Sundays. But this attorney also deserves our sympathy, for Count Fathom's mode of paying his lawyer's bill was to split the poor attorney's head with a poker, and when remonstrated with by the doctor—who took a grave view of the possible result of his violence—his reply is significant of the estimation in which, in Smollett's day, the attorney was held.

I am not so unacquainted with the resistance of an attorney's skull as to believe the chastisement I have inflicted upon him will at all endanger his life, which is in much greater danger from the hands of the common executioner.

Fielding had no exalted opinion of the
solicitors of his day, although, as a member
of the bar, he must have looked to them for
briefs.   His opinion is quaintly expressed in
his left-handed compliment to Mr. Dowling,
the attorney in " Tom Jones," of whom it is
quaintly remarked that " he had not divested
himself of humanity in being an attorney."

In " Man and Wife " Wilkie Collins presents two colourless solicitors described as
belonging to—

That large class of purely *mechanical* and perfectly
mediocre persons connected with the practice of the law,
who will probably, in a more advanced state of society,
be superseded by machinery.

This description of the colourless type of
lawyer is, in suggestiveness, worthy of
Dickens himself.

Perhaps the most optimistic view of the
lawyer in modern fiction is that in Sir
Walter Besant's legal novel " The Ivory

Gate," a book which contains quite a number
of legal characters, and not a bad one
amongst them.   His portrait of a solicitor
is in refreshing contrast to some of those
I have quoted.

The solicitor is always engaged in considering how
best to guide his fellow-man through the labyrinthine
world.   He receives his fellow-man at his entrance into
life as a ward; he receives him grown up as a client;
he advises him all his life, at every step, and in every
emergency.   If the client goes into partnership, or
marries, or buys a house, or builds one, or gets into
trouble, the solicitor advises and assists him.   When
the client grows old, the solicitor makes his will.   When
the client dies, the solicitor becomes executor and his
trustee, and administers his estate.   It is thus a life
spent entirely for other people.   I know not of any other
profession, unless it be medicine, that so much can be
said of.   And think what terrors, what anxieties, what
disappointments the solicitor witnesses and alleviates.
Think of the family scandals he hushes up and keeps
secret.   Good Heavens! if a solicitor in large practice
were to tell what he knows, think of the terrible
disclosures!   He knows everything.   He knows more
than a Roman Catholic priest, because his penitents not
only reveal their own sins, but also those of their wives,
and sons, and friends, and partners.

This humorously sarcastic picture strikes just the note which explains the frequent use of the lawyer on the stage and in fiction. The many-sidedness of the profession of the law lends itself to the most varied treatment. Nothing in the way of knowledge (especially knowledge of so-called secrets) is so deep, and nothing in the way of behaviour is so eccentric, but a lawyer can be made to fit the part, and so it is not surprising that the pages of fiction teem with lawyers, and that no melodrama is complete without a stage lawyer in rusty black.

Perhaps the most lovable of all lawyers in fiction are those in Thackeray's "Pendennis"; and in " Philip " he presents us in Mr. Bond, of Bond & Selby, with a unique type of lawyer who had the courage to quarrel with his best client.

In " Perlycross " Mr. Blackmore presents Mr. Webber, a family solicitor, who was "no time server, only bound by his duty to the firm and his sense of loyal service to a client."

In "Thicker than Water" Mr. James Payn introduces a solicitor with a high sense of honour and no small amount of professional courage, who, to his own loss, sacrificed a client for whom he refused to make a will which was palpably unjust; but he had this satisfaction, that the will, being executed by a rival solicitor, was afterwards found to be invalid.

In "The Castle Inn" of Mr. Stanley Weyman Mr. Peter Fishwick is another example in fiction of the poor but honest attorney.

Instances might be multiplied indefinitely of novels in which the law and the lawyer play a part, I had almost said in which the law is dragged in and the lawyer is made to act a part, for in a vast number of instances the novelist's ideas about what the

law is are exceedingly amusing. Plots are
evolved out of legal situations which could
never occur, and lawyers are represented as
saying and doing things which no sane
lawyer in real life would ever dream of
saying or doing. It has often struck me
that some young lawyer with time on his
hands might do his profession a service, and
amuse the public, by compiling a volume
of extracts from popular novels setting
forth the law as expressed in the novels,
and in a parallel column the law as
it really is. Often the law is regarded
as a subject with which the novelist
may take a wide licence and may present
legal principles and legal practices, not
as they really exist, but as the exigencies
of the tale, and the evolution of the
plot, require. I do not suppose anybody
wants a serious view of the law presented in
the pages of a novel, for the law student

does not go there for his legal principles, or
to inform himself of the correct practice of
the Courts; and the real view of the law, as
applied to the circumstances created by the
novelist, would very often be sordid and
uninteresting, whilst imaginative law, in
the hands of a clever writer, can be made
interesting, and sometimes even exciting.

After all, the view of the law which so
often prevails in fiction is true to human
experience, for the bulk of humanity—
especially that portion of it which has
escaped falling into the toils of the law as a
personal experience—looks at the matter
broadly and regards the profession col-
lectively. It is not uncommon in every-
day life to hear disparaging comment
on the legal profession, made by people
who, if caught up sharply, and pinned down
to give a concrete instance of what they talk
vaguely about as the sharp practices of

B

lawyers, are, to their own surprise perhaps,
obliged to admit that the individual lawyers
they do happen to know personally, do not at
all answer to their general idea of the class.
On the stage, and in the pages of fiction, a
lawyer is very seldom what is called a
"popular" character.   The stage lawyer is
often the villain of the piece.   Seldom is he
presented as a benefactor, or a model of
virtuous honesty, or the champion of the
oppressed, or the exponent of the truth.
Such a stage lawyer would probably be
condemned as unreal by the critical playgoer.
And yet, is it not, in real life, the case that
the high-souled lawyer is a real personage, as
many have (perhaps to their own surprise)
discovered in their time of stress and mis-
fortune?   In one of his books Anthony
Trollope aptly says :

Is it not remarkable that the common repute which
we all give to attorneys in general is exactly opposite to

that which every man gives to his own attorney in particular? Whom does anybody trust so implicitly as he trusts his own attorney, and yet is it not the case that the body of attorneys is supposed to be the most roguish body in existence?

But if the lawyer has been unjustly maligned in literature, he may console himself that he is not alone. The other professions have suffered in the same way. As regards the Church, is not fiction full of pictures of the lazy and the hypocritical parson? As regards medicine, have not doctors been brutally caricatured as quacks who "thrust drugs of which they know little into bodies of which they know less"? And is not such criticism the outcome of the same baneful tendency to generalise, and subject to the same curious anomaly, that the critic who indulges in the cheap sneer at the body, is often the earnest believer in the individual? Outside of the professions the same mis-description prevails in literature.

Are not many novels built upon imaginary
mercantile transactions which, as the business
world is constituted, would be simply
impossible in real life, and have not
merchants and traders and others been
traduced for the purposes of sensational
fiction? Dr. Johnson's crabbed definition of
a stockbroker as "a low wretch who gets his
money by buying and selling shares in the
funds," is as much out of harmony with the
truth as are many imaginary definitions in
fiction of the parson, or the doctor, or the
lawyer.

But I am at present more particularly
concerned only with Dickens' attitude
towards the law, and with the lawyer as
painted by Dickens. His method is not the
common one of unreasoning denunciation of
a class. He knew better than to represent
all lawyers as rogues, for he had the
advantage of knowing the legal profession

from the inside. He never lays down bad
law, and he never credits a member of the
legal profession with impossible professional
conduct.

But even Dickens could not divest himself
of the common habit of allowing personal
experience to colour his views. The plunger
who, in his haste to be rich, stakes and loses
on the Stock Exchange, immediately pro-
ceeds to revile his stockbroker, whose only
interest in the business was the earning of a
modest commission. Smarting under the
loss of money in an unfortunate speculation,
the client is ready to adopt Dr. Johnson's
definition of a stockbroker. So also the man
who is unfortunate in his appeal to the law
is often too ready to say with Mr. Bumble,
the parochial beadle in "Oliver Twist," that
"the law is a ass—a idiot." Every lawyer
knows only too well that the layman
is too apt to form his opinions of the

law generally according as the law has been kind or has been cruel to him personally; and so, in regarding the legal scenes and characters in Dickens' works, it is useful always to bear in mind that Dickens did not love the law. Nor was his resentment a passing phase. His hatred of the Court of Chancery began with his own experience as a suitor. He was involved in a Chancery lawsuit over the piracy of his "Christmas Carol" and "Martin Chuzzlewit." He was entirely successful, for the lawsuit resulted in the pirates making a public apology. The judgment of the Court also found them liable in costs, but unfortunately the costs were not recovered, and Dickens had the not uncommon experience of securing a victory at law, but having himself to pay for it. In the first blush of his victory he wrote exuberantly :

The pirates are beaten flat. They are bruised,

bloody, battered, smashed, squelched, and utterly undone.

But when his bill of costs came in, and the pirates went insolvent, and could not pay, his exuberance was modified. There is nothing so effective in modifying exuberant jollity as a lawyer's bill. Dickens—like many another litigant—visited upon the Court the sins of the opposing litigant. It was not the fault of the Court that the pirates could not pay the costs, but Dickens counted it against the Court nevertheless, and when, within a couple of years, he again experienced piracy, he preferred to bear the ills he had rather than fly to others that, as regards the attendant cost, he knew not of. Once bitten, twice shy. He declined again to resort to the law, and wrote thus bitterly of his former experience :

I shall not easily forget the expense, and anxiety, *and horrible injustice* of the " Carol " case.

Strong language is excusable on the part of a litigant who fights a lawsuit and loses it, and has to pay for the losing of it. Still stronger excuse is there for the ire of the man who fights a lawsuit, and gains it, and has to pay the costs of gaining it. But what may seem at the time injustice and anxiety are forgettable elements. Even the expense in time the average suitor can forget. But Dickens never forgot. This early experience coloured not only his opinion of the Chancery Court, but his opinion of the law generally. Thirty years later, in a private letter—and that, too, a letter to a lady—he wrote :

> I have that high opinion of the law of England generally which one is likely to derive from the impression that it puts all the honest men under the diabolical hoofs of all the scoundrels. It makes me *cautious of doing right*—an admirable instance of its wisdom.

This sweeping sarcastic comment indicates that his attitude towards the whole judicial system was hostile, and, I venture to think, somewhat unreasonable. That there were abuses in his day, as there are in the present day, goes without saying. No system of law is incapable of abuse. In all his works Dickens no doubt aimed at calling public attention to abuses, with the hope of their being remedied, and in this instance, as in others, that aim was good. But even the greatest men are at times small, and, in this matter, it seems very plain that he was in such a novel as " Bleak House" working off his personal hatred of the Chancery Court of England, as well as showing up the abuses to which the practice of that Court lent itself.

The greatest novel of the law which Dickens produced—the most effective tale of the law, I think, ever written—was " Bleak House." It begins and ends in the Court of Chancery, and there is—from beginning to end of the long tale—not a single

character who can be said to be outside of
the influence of the dominating legal element.
In some of his other books the law plays an
important part, but it only plays a part.
There are other parts to play, and other
interests to introduce. But in " Bleak
House " the atmosphere of the law prevails
throughout. Judges and Chancery Court
officials, barristers, solicitors, law clerks, law
stationers, detectives and police inspectors,
litigants, singly or in groups, always occupy
the stage, and every incident of the tale has
a legal environment. Perhaps this very fact
explains why " Bleak House," although, as I
at least think, the most powerful sustained
effort which Dickens made, is not his most
popular novel. The legal characters are
perhaps more subtly drawn, but they do not
stand out of the canvas in the same way as,
for instance, the popular legal characters in
the " Pickwick Papers." To the experienced

lawyer there is a very subtle humour in the interminable arguments of the Chancery barristers in the suit upon which the tale in " Bleak House " is built ; but the humour is often missed by the lay reader, who more readily understands the lawyers of the " Pick- wick Papers." The deferential Chancery solicitors of " Bleak House " are, from a professional point of view, perhaps more interesting studies of legal character than bustling practitioners like Perker, or Dodson & Fogg of " Pickwick." But to the general reader they do not appeal. Mr. Tangle, K.C., and Kenge & Carboy, the Chancery solicitors of " Bleak House," will never grip the public imagination like Sergeant Buzfuz and Dodson & Fogg of " Pickwick." All that he knew of the law and of the Law Courts Dickens put into " Bleak House." The plot itself is not an original one in its inception, but its development and its finish are new. Many lawsuits have been described in the pages of fiction, but never one like *Jarndyce and Jarndyce*, the Chancery suit which in the opening chapter is described as "that scarecrow of a suit which has in course of time become so complicated that no man alive knows what it means." This lawsuit drove some of the parties to it into their graves, and others into lunatic asylums ; and in the end fittingly died of inanition, the whole estate which was the subject of the litigation having melted away in costs.

I think that Dickens was too hard upon the Chancery Court. As I have said, his vision of it was coloured by his own unfortunate experience. But the moral of "Bleak House," nevertheless, was not unneeded—although morals, where most needed, not infrequently are most unheeded. The

law's delay is an old grievance, and it is
to be feared that no system of legal
procedure can ever entirely avoid that.   But
the methods of all British Courts of law
have vastly improved since Dickens' day, and
the improvements in Chancery Court practice
probably owe more than its officials would
care to admit to the exposure of the judicial
methods which Dickens made in " Bleak
House."   In his enthusiasm for reform, however, Dickens forgot that if there were no
litigants there would be no lawsuits, and that
Courts of law are very often what litigants
make them.   It is a common experience
that illustrated so gloomily throughout this
book—the effort of a litigant to extract for
himself something out of a lawsuit which he
would have been well advised never to have
entered upon, and then, when his efforts have
resulted in nothing, the tendency of the
litigant, not to blame himself for entering

upon a wild-goose chase, but rather to blame the judge, or the Court system, or his own lawyers, or the opposing lawyers, or anything, or anybody, other than himself.

The picture of the Court of Chancery upon a foggy November day, with which "Bleak House" opens, has never been equalled as a setting of judicial environment. The descriptions of Courts in novels are often as imaginative as the law in them.

Dickens knew the Courts too well to fall into the common error of laying his Court scenes in a false setting. In his early days he had opportunities of studying the solemnities of the law, first, as a youth in the office of Messrs. Ellis & Blackmore, later, as a junior law clerk in the office of Mr. Molloy, of 6 Symonds' Inn, who was the prototype of Mr. Vholes, the solicitor for Richard Carstone in the " Bleak

House" Chancery suit, and later still as a shorthand Court reporter. He had himself also at one time the idea of becoming a barrister, and actually kept a few terms in one of the Inns of Court, but he abandoned the legal profession for that of literature. Dickens also had many lawyer friends, and numbered amongst his intimates such men as Talfourd, Denman, Campbell, and Hawkins.

In daily association with the judicial solemnities, it was impossible for him, even when setting out to caricature the Chancery Court system, to present other than a realistic picture of the Chancery Court itself. In all Dickens' writings I know of nothing which better illustrates that natural capacity of his for absorbing small details, which is the great charm of his descriptions of places and people, than the brief description of the Chancery Court in the opening chapter of " Bleak House." The Court itself, " dim with wasting candles here and there," the Lord Chancellor on the bench, "with a foggy glory round his head softly fenced in with crimson cloth and curtains." This judge, and Justice Starleigh, who presided at the Pickwick trial, are Dickens' two contrast pictures of the bench. The Lord Chancellor in "Bleak House" is always courteous and polished, and betrays nothing of the boredom which the case of *Jarndyce and Jarndyce* was bound to inflict. He is courteous to Mr. Tangle, K.C., the "large advocate with great whiskers and a little voice." He is courteous also to "a very little counsel with a terrific bass voice, who arises fully inflated in the back settlements of the fog." Still more courteous is the Lord Chancellor receiving the two young wards in his own room. To this judge Dickens has as kindly a leaning as he, by contrast, had an unkindly feeling to Justice Starleigh.

In his Court, and about this judge, the atmosphere of diginity which surrounds the Chancellor is altogether absent.

Mr. Justice Starleigh was a most particularly short man, and so fat that he seemed all face and waistcoat. He rolled in upon two little turned legs, and having bobbed gravely to the bar, who bobbed gravely to him, put his little legs underneath his table, and his little three-cornered hat upon it, and when Mr. Justice Starleigh had done this, all you could see of him was two queer little eyes, one broad pink face, and somewhere about half of a very big and very comical-looking wig.

Speaking of judges generally in his "American Notes," Dickens voices a very common idea of Courts of law. Many people can never dissociate the idea of stage effect from a Court. These people regard a Court as a set scene, in which every one has a set part to take; and perhaps in a sense they are not far wrong, for there is an absence of individualism about a law Court. For the time being the barrister is not him-

c

self, but his client, looking at things from the client's point of view ; for the time being the judge is not an individual with personal opinions, but is the embodiment of the law, for the making of which he is not responsible, but only for its application. In the "American Notes" Dickens makes this quaint remark :

There is undoubtedly a degree of protection in the wig and gown, a dismissal of individual responsibility in dressing for the part.

To Dickens himself, the irascible little judge whom he created to preside at the trial of *Bardell* v. *Pickwick* had a special fascination. Justice Starleigh was one of his own creations whom he loved to impersonate. In that recently-published delightful book by R. C. Lehmann, entitled "Memories of Half a Century," there is described a reading given by Dickens of the Pickwick trial scene, in the course of which Mr. Lehmann says :

I shall never forget my amazement when Dickens assumed the character of Mr. Justice Starleigh. The face and figure that I knew, that I had seen on the stage a moment before, seemed to vanish as if by magic, and there appeared instead a fat, pompous, pursy little man with a plump imbecile face from which every vestige of good temper and cheerfulness, everything, in fact, except an expression of self-sufficient stupidity, had been removed. The upper lip had become long, the corners of the mouth drooped, the nose was short and podgy, all the angles of the chin had gone, the chin itself had receded into the throat, and the eyes, lately so humorous and human, had become as malicious and obstinate as those of a pig. It was a marvellous effect in transformation.

Nevertheless, Justice Starleigh is the familiar friend of every Dickens reader, whilst the polished Lord Chancellor lives in the recollection of but few.

Of the three leading solicitors of "Bleak House," two are of a somewhat characterless type. They are both in Chancery practice, which does not seem to lend itself to any great individuality of character. "Conversation Kenge," as he was called, of the firm of Kenge & Carboy, the solicitors for Mr. Jarndyce, is but a more successful and therefore a more cheerful edition of the melancholy Mr. Vholes, the solicitor for Richard Carstone. In Dickens' books the names of his characters are often full of significance. Mr. Vholes is an instance of that, a "vole" in a card game meaning a deal where all the winning cards fall to the dealer. It was in "Bleak House" that Dickens said, "The one great principle of the English law is to make business for itself." Solicitors created upon this low estimate of their profession, could not well be particularly interesting. The Chancery solicitors of "Bleak House" are none of them very lovable characters. They are too respectable and too commonplace. Take, for instance, the portrait of Mr. Vholes.

Mr. Vholes is a very respectable man. He has not a very large business, but he is a very respectable man.

He is allowed by the greater attorneys who have made
good fortunes, or are making them, to be a most
respectable man. He never misses a chance in his
practice, which is a mark of respectability; he never
takes any pleasure, which is another mark of respectability; he is reserved and serious, which is also a mark
of respectability; his digestion is impaired, which is
highly respectable; he is making hay of the grass which
is flesh, for his three daughters and his father are
dependent on him in the Vale of Taunton.

The third . leading solicitor of " Bleak
House " is a very marked contrast to the
other two.   There is nothing commonplace
about Mr. Tulkinghorn, the family solicitor
of Sir Leicester Dedlock, and the confidential depositary of the secrets of the great.
Mr. Tulkinghorn of Lincoln's Inn Fields is,
in my opinion, by far the most finished
creation amongst all the Dickens lawyers.
This lawyer tersely, but comprehensively,
defined as "an oyster of the old school
whom nobody can open," combines an
old-school courtesy with the ferreting

proclivities of a Scotland Yard detective. From the time he appears at old Crooks' rag store, in search of information about the poverty-stricken law writer, till his dramatic end by being shot, the action of the story turns upon him even more than upon the Chancery suit itself.

In "Bleak House," lower down in the professional scale, we find a greater wealth of character than amongst the barristers or attorneys, and, in real human interest, none of the legal characters approaches to "the young man of the name of Guppy," the law clerk of Kenge & Carboy. As a study in law life he is most interesting. He first appears when sent by Mr. Kenge to meet the Chancery wards, and he is introduced in a few brief words, descriptive of the office boy of all time—"a young gentleman who had inked himself by accident." He rapidly developed under the influence

of these "chords in the human heart" which
it was his gloomy delight to strike. His
proposal of marriage to Miss Summerson,
"without prejudice," is in the best vein of
Dickens humour.

We read in the Life of Dickens how
vividly he realised the characters he was
creating—how he laughed aloud as the comic
creations grew under his pen—how he wept
as he chronicled sadness. I often think with
what delight he must have painted the portrait of "the young man of the name of
Guppy." Dickens could enter into the
feelings of just such a young man, for he had
himself been a young law clerk, and he had
a real love for the law clerk who figures in
so many of his books, and of whom he had
never an unkind word to say.

There are several grades of lawyer's clerks. There
is the articled clerk who has paid a premium, and
is an attorney in perspective, who runs a tailor's bill,

receives invitations to parties, knows a family in Gower Street and another in Tavistock Square, who goes out of town every long vacation to see his father who keeps innumerable horses, and who is, in short, the very aristocrat of clerks.

When David Copperfield was articled to Spenlow & Jorkins, his aunt, Betsy Trotwood, had to put down a premium of £1000 for him, and he got no salary.

Then there is the salaried clerk—out-of-door or indoor as the case may be—who devotes the major part of his thirty shillings a week to his personal pleasure and adornments, repairs half-price to the Adelphi Theatre at least three times a week, dissipates majestically at the cider cellars afterwards, and is a dirty caricature of the fashion which expired six months ago. Then there is the middle-aged copying clerk who is always shabby and often drunk, and there are the office lads in their first surtouts, who feel a befitting contempt for boys at day schools, club as they go home at night for saveloys and porter, and think there's nothing like life.

" The young man of the name of Guppy " belonged to the better class of salaried clerk,

but he had ambition beyond that sphere, and
he was appreciated by his employers, for we
find him, in the closing chapter of the book,
able to represent to Miss Summerson in
pressing his suit that he had now been
presented with his articles by Kenge &
Carboy, and so was on the first rung of the
ladder towards being a Chancery practitioner.
The "chords in the human heart" are the
attributes of "the young man of the name of
Guppy" which the general reader of "Bleak
House" mostly recollects. But his love
story was only one side of Mr. Guppy—not
all of him, and other and suggestive aspects
of his nature are disclosed by such episodes
as the way he stood by his friend Tony
Jobling, who had gone down hill, the part
he took in unearthing the secret of Lady
Dedlock and Miss Summerson, his devotion
to Miss Summerson, at whose request he
desisted from investigating the clue he had,

and his kindness to and firm belief in his
mother. I am persuaded that Charles
Dickens intended "the young man of the
name of Guppy" to go down to posterity a
type in his own sphere of one of Nature's
gentlemen, who, as a law clerk, was faithful
to his employer's interests, and also ambi-
tious for his own advancement in the
profession ; who, as a lover, was constant to
"the image enshrined upon his heart," and
who in general was an all-round good
fellow.

In "Bleak House" the law takes on a
sombre aspect, but in the "Pickwick Papers"
the whole legal aspect is cheerful. None
of the lawyers there is tinged with melancholy. They are all of the lively and
cheerful sort. Take Perker, for instance,
Mr. Pickwick's own legal adviser—

A little high-dried man with a dark squeezed-up face
and small restless black eyes, that kept winking and

twinkling on each side of his little inquisitive nose, as if they were playing a perpetual game of peep-bo with that feature. He was dressed all in black, with boots as shiny as his eyes, a low white neckcloth and a clean shirt with a frill to it. A gold watch chain and seals depended from his fob. He carried his black kid gloves *in* his hands, not *on* them, and as he spoke, thrust his wrists beneath his coat-tails with the air of a man who was in the habit of propounding some regular posers.

Is not Perker the familiar type of the self-confident, but not brilliant, legal adviser, who is as well known in legal circles now as then? But before Dodson & Fogg Perker pales in legal interest. Although Dickens' only contribution to the literature of the law had been his creation of Dodson & Fogg, he would have taken a first place as the portrayer of legal character. The hold upon the public imagination which this firm has acquired is wonderful. An illustration of this realism occurred not very long ago, when a jury awarded to a solicitor

damages against a client who had called him
"a regular Dodson & Fogg."

From the lawyer's point of view one
is tempted to inquire whether, after all,
the commonly accepted view of Dodson
& Fogg is warranted. They have been
held up to ignominy as unscrupulous petti-
foggers, and they will probably continue to
be so regarded. But a lawyer does not
create the facts of a case. He gets them
from his client, and Mrs. Bardell's case was
undoubtedly, as put before her solicitors, a
good jury case. It is a striking thing that
the evidence upon which she got a
verdict was entirely the evidence of Mr.
Pickwick's own friends. Mr. Winkle, Mr.
Tupman, and Mr. Snodgrass were all what
lawyers call "hostile witnesses." So was
Sam Weller. The jury, of course, knew
that they were the defendant's own friends,
and no kind of evidence so tells with a jury

as admissions wrung in cross-examination
from a reluctant friend witness. In a case
of the sort, what damaging admissions these
friends had to make! Dodson & Fogg
were acute practitioners who astutely refrained from overdoing their case. They
contented themselves with proving their case
out of the mouths of Mr. Pickwick's own
friends. It was not buttressed by what we
call collateral evidence. Mr. Pickwick's
experiences would not have been difficult
to trace. What if Dodson & Fogg
had, for instance, called his friend Mr.
Wardle and others to speak to Mr. Pickwick's general behaviour? Of course we
know that the kissing of ladies, old and
young, and being kissed by them, was all
part of the general jollity at the hospitable
Wardle's country home. Of course we all
know that there was nothing but benevolent
intention in Mr. Pickwick's being found at

midnight in the grounds of a young ladies' boarding school.   Of course we know that it was entirely owing to a geographical error that Mr. Pickwick found himself in a lady's bedroom in the hotel at Ipswich.   But the jury did not know all this, and such circumstances would have been quite relevant to make out a general character for frivolity and gallantry against the unfortunate Pickwick.   The general character of the defendant is a not unimportant element in such cases, and Dodson & Fogg might have disclosed much more than they did to influence a jury.   That they did not attempt this certainly stamps them as experienced lawyers, who knew when they had a good case in brief compass, and so refrained from making the very common error of overlaying such a case, with the possible result of strangling it.   Then, in such cases, the demeanour of the parties is

always an element with the jury. A view of
the plaintiff commonly entertained is that
she was a fat and by no means attractive
elderly female, but the well-known picture by
Browne of Mrs. Bardell fainting away and
being discovered in Mr. Pickwick's arms by
his three friends represents her as a plump
and comely widow, and it is quite likely that
at the trial the personal appearance of the
distressed plaintiff had its due weight with
the jury. If she had not been comely
Dodson & Fogg were certainly too astute to
have presented her in Court. There was
ample evidence to support the verdict of the
jury. If it had not been so, Perker would
no doubt have applied for a new trial. But he
recognised that the evidence was sufficient,
for he accepted the verdict.

Dickens wrote before the days when it
was competent to examine the parties in
their own suits. In present-day practice,

the leading features of a breach of promise suit are the examination of the fair plaintiff, and the cross-examination of the perturbed defendant. What a pity that was not permissible in Dickens' day. What cross-examination Mr. Pickwick would have been subjected to by Serjeant Buzfuz, and how Pickwick would have lost his temper and given his case away. But Dickens was too loyal to the law to put Mr. Pickwick into the witness-box in the book, when he could not have done so in the Court itself. He contented himself with putting into the speech of Serjeant Buzfuz the points which could, with telling effect, have been made the basis of a cross-examination scene.

There seems therefore nothing out of the ordinary course as regards the conduct of the trial. The subsequent behaviour of Dodson & Fogg was in accordance with the ideas of the time. Of course, looking at it from our twentieth-century point of view, it may appear monstrous that Mr. Pickwick should have been incarcerated because he refused to implement the jury's verdict, and possibly still more monstrous that Mrs. Bardell also should have found herself in the Fleet because she would not pay Dodson & Fogg's costs. But we have to recollect that, in Dickens' day, a debtor who failed to pay his debt could, as the law expressed it, have his person taken in execution. Even at the present time people are sent to prison every day because they will not pay certain kinds of debt. No doubt the incarceration of a debtor who is unable to pay his creditor is always hard. But no such element existed in Mr. Pickwick's case. Upon the verdict of the jury the Court had adjudged him debtor to Mrs. Bardell for the damages awarded, and debtor to Dodson & Fogg

D

for their costs.   Mr. Pickwick was quite
able to pay, and it was, accordingly, Dodson & Fogg's professional duty to their
client to recover her damages, and their duty
to themselves to recover their costs.   To
effect this they were doing no more than the
law permitted when they put Mr. Pickwick—
and ultimately Mrs. Bardell herself—into the
Fleet.   Their anxiety to recover their costs
the general reader does not appreciate, and
perhaps Dickens' own experience of law
costs in the piracy case before referred to,
which rankled in his mind, may have led
him unconsciously to unduly emphasise the
element of the costs, and to forget that, after
all, a lawyer's bill is a debt just as much as a
tailor's bill.

It is a tendency of lay human nature to
regard a lawyer's bill as somehow different
from any other kind of debt.   There are
some people who have an idea that a lawyer

should be the benefactor, as well as the
adviser, of his client, that when a litigation
has been lost, for instance, the lawyer
should not press for his costs, and that at
any rate there is never any hurry for
paying a lawyer's bill. The prevalence
of ideas of that sort, and the popular
suspicion of the law entertained by so
large a proportion of humanity, probably
explain why Dodson & Fogg have, in
the public mind, became synonymous with
chicanery and harsh dealing; but upon a
fair and impartial weighing of their recorded
sayings and doings there may be room for
some doubt as to whether they have not
been unjustly vilified.

I have always wondered whether Dickens
himself ever contemplated that Dodson &
Fogg would come to be associated in the
public mind with all that is mean and tricky
in the practice of the law. I am inclined to

think that he did not, and that he really had in his mind a much broader aim than merely to pillory the speculative lawyer, who has existed in all time, and exists to-day, and is not without his uses in the legal world. The history of the famous lawsuit of *Bardell* v. *Pickwick* was, I think, intended to be taken as a whole, and, so regarded, it is a delightful piece of satire upon the laws of evidence and the practice of trial by jury. It sometimes happens that a particular incident or a particular character in a tale takes such a hold upon the public mind that the author's broader aim is lost sight of, and it is possibly so in this instance. Dodson & Fogg so catch the fancy that some readers never get past them, and forget that there were other characters and other elements in the little drama, and so they miss the delicate satire of this episode in the genial Pickwick's career. Incidentally, the author no doubt intended to condemn the conduct of litigation upon a speculative basis, and also to illustrate how, in the hands of clever lawyers, incidents, trifling and innocent in themselves, may be made to appear fraught with deep meaning, and be presented to a credulous, and possibly not over-intelligent, jury as what lawyers call "circumstantial evidence." But these were only incidents. The broad aim of the author was to present an object-lesson designed to cast ridicule upon that legal system which he so much detested, and which he never missed an opportunity of holding up to scorn.

There is yet another lawyer in "Pickwick Papers" who deserves special mention, for he is of a type quite distinct from either Kenge & Carboy or Dodson & Fogg. Solomon Pell was of the fraternity known as bar-parlour lawyers, who practised in the Insolvent Court, now abolished as a separate institution and merged in the Bankruptcy

Court.   These parlour lawyers Dickens
thus described :

> The professional establishment of the more opulent of
> these gentlemen consists of a blue bag and a boy.   They
> have no fixed offices, their legal business being transacted
> in the parlours of public-houses or the yards of prisons.

Mr. Solomon Pell had two of the essential
elements which make for success in the law—
he had perfect confidence in himself, and he
had the art of inspiring confidence in his clients.
One of his clients was Mr. Weller, senior,
who first met him over obtaining the
discharge of a friend of the road " who had
contracted a speculative but improvident
passion for horsing long stages, which had
led to his present embarrassments."   Mr.
Pell had then so impressed Mr. Weller
that, when he and Sam conceived the idea
of having Sam arrested for debt, so that
he might go into the Fleet to be near Mr.
Pickwick, Mr. Weller at once resorted to

Mr. Pell, whom he thus described to Sam :
" A limb o' the law, Sammy, as has got
brains like the frogs, dispersed all over his
body, and reachin' to the very tips of his
fingers."

Mr. Pell was fortunate in retaining this
client's confidence for all kinds of business,
for after Sam had made his father understand
that legal formalities were required to prove
the late Mrs. Weller's will, Mr. Weller had
no hesitation about the selection of his
lawyer : " Pell must look into this, Sammy.
He's the man for a difficult question of law."
And this piece of business being satisfactorily
disposed of, Mr. Weller and his professional
adviser parted with mutual regard, their
farewell, like their introduction, being made
in the bar-parlour, and their confidence
in each other remaining unshaken. Mr.
Solomon Pell, like all the lawyers of
" Pickwick," took a cheerful view of life,

although the phase of it which came particularly under his notice did not inspire cheerfulness. But ingress and exit at the Fleet required the aid of the law. Insolvent debtors were not particular as to the personality of their lawyers, and till the Fleet was closed these bar-parlour lawyers were a necessary evil, and, in their own sphere, perhaps, served their clients as usefully as more exalted practitioners in the more savoury regions of legal practice.

In "Great Expectations" we make the acquaintance of a different phase of the law, and of two of the best of Dickens' legal creations—Mr. Jaggers and his clerk, the cheerful Mr. Wemmick. Of every other lawyer in the Dickens collection we have a personal description ; of Mr. Jaggers we have none, and yet his personality is vivid. No reader of " Great Expectations " can rise from its perusal without feeling that this

character, in regard to whom the fewest words
are said, is yet the outstanding personality of
the tale.   When he first appears upon the
scene, visiting Pip to tell him of his good
fortune, Mr. Jaggers thus tersely introduces
himself, and in so doing reveals the man :

My name is Jaggers, and I am a lawyer in London.
I am pretty well known.

Equally laconic, but quite expressive, is
Mr. Wemmick's description of his master :

Always seems to me as if he had set a man-trap and
was watching it.   Suddenly—click—you're caught.

Upon Pip remarking that he supposed Mr.
Jaggers was a skilful lawyer—"Deep," said
Wemmick, "as Australia," pointing with
his pen at the office floor to express that
Australia was understood for the purpose
of the figure to be symmetrically on the
opposite spot of the globe.   "If there was

anything deeper," added Wemmick, "*he'd be it.*" As to the methods of business of some criminal lawyers, how a few words may express much, is illustrated by the following brief but suggestive conversation between Mr. Jaggers and his tout Mike, the "gentleman with one eye, in a velveteen suit and fur cap." This is the conversation :

"Oh," said Mr. Jaggers, turning to the man who was pulling a lock of hair in the middle of his forehead, like the bull in Cock Robin pulling at the bell rope, "your man comes on this afternoon. Well?" "Well, Master Jaggers," returned Mike in the voice of a sufferer from a constitutional cold, "arter a deal of trouble I found one, sir, as might do." "What is he prepared to swear?" "Well, Master Jaggers," said Mike, wiping his nose on his fur cap, "in a general way, *anythink.*"

Pip's impression of Mr. Jaggers when he went to see him in the Court is thus recorded :

He had a woman under examination, or cross-examination—I don't know which—and was striking her, and the bench, and everybody, with awe. If anybody of whosoever degree said a word that he didn't approve,

he instantly required to have it *taken down.* If anybody wouldn't make an admission, he said, "I'll have
it out of you," and if anybody made an admission, he said,
"Now I have got you." The magistrates shivered under
a single bite of his finger. Thieves and thief-takers hung
in dread rapture on his words, and shrank when a hair of
his eyebrows turned in their direction. Which side he was
on I couldn't make out, for he seemed to me to be
grinding the whole place in a mill.

Dickens had a wonderful power of interpreting impressions. This description exactly personates the criminal lawyer. The man who devotes himself exclusively to criminal practice often acquires an Esau-like attitude of mind. For the time his hand seems to be against every man. He comes instinctively to regard every adverse witness as a liar, and about all great criminal lawyers there is an indescribable quality which compels attention, and inspires not only the confidence of clients, but the fearing respect of all regular frequenters of the criminal Courts.

Mr. Jaggers is not a pleasant character.

He was not meant to be. He was meant to portray a special type of lawyer, better known in London than elsewhere, for London is the home of the specialised lawyer. And Mr. Jaggers is the type of the Old Bailey practitioner, the only one in all Dickens' writings, and introduced, as I think, in this book specially to represent this type, for the tale did not necessarily require a criminal lawyer; for the purposes of the story any kind of confidential lawyer would have sufficed.

In pleasing contrast to the hard and sour Mr. Jaggers, who so markedly took on the character of his surroundings, is his genial confidential clerk Mr. Wemmick, whom no surroundings influenced, whose domestic pleasantries so contrasted with his professional duties, with his toy of a house at Walworth, "the Castle" which was the pride of his deaf old father—"the aged P." Wemmick is the Mark Tapley of the law.

The sordidness of his professional employ-
ment could not damp his spirits. He had
grasped the philosophy of the entire separation
of the professional and domestic side of life
when he said to Pip :

> The office is one thing, and private life is another :
> when I go into the office, I leave the Castle behind me,
> and when I come into the Castle, I leave the office
> behind me.

To do just this is a most difficult thing
for a busy lawyer to do. But that it is
difficult to follow in practice does not make
Mr. Wemmick's philosophy of professional
life the less sound.

In " Our Mutual Friend " the law plays
little part. Mortimer Lightwood, no
doubt, was a lawyer, and so was his friend
Eugene Wrayburn. But their practice of
the law was but nominal, and their aim in
life was the pursuit of pleasure rather than
of guineas. They were, however, like all

the Dickens lawyers, typical of their class. They represent the type of lawyer who takes a legal qualification rather for its social than its professional aspect, and there is nothing about them of any distinct professional character.

In "The Mystery of Edwin Drood" there is only one lawyer, and he also is typical of his class, that select class of the semi-retired professional man who with a legal training has drifted into a legal siding, and smothered professional ambition.

Mr. Grewgious had been bred to the bar and had laid himself out for chamber practice, to draw deeds—"'convey' the wise it call," as Pistol says. But conveyancing and he had made such a very indifferent marriage of it that they separated by consent, if there can be said to be separation where there had never been coming together. No, coy conveyancing would not come to Mr. Grewgious. She was wooed, not won, and they went their several ways. But an arbitration being blown towards him by some unaccountable wind, and he gaining great credit in it, as one indefatigable in seeking out right, and doing right, a pretty fat receivership was next blown into his pocket, by a wind more traceable to its source. So by chance he had found his niche.

I always think of Grewgious as a suspended Perker. Perhaps he never had any great ambition to get on in his profession. Many lawyers do lack a real interest in their profession, and so they do not advance in it. Mr. Grewgious was this sort of lawyer, not to be called a failure exactly, but rather a might-have-been. Of course a comfortable appointment is a very pleasant form in which to suffer professional ambition to be smothered, and Mr. Grewgious in his niche is a pleasing picture of content. But he ceases to be interesting as a lawyer. Dickens tersely sums him up thus :

> He had snuffed out his ambition (supposing him to have ever lighted it) and had settled down with his snuffers for the rest of his life.

There, as the lawyer, we leave Mr. Grewgious. We are not here concerned with him in his character of the kind-hearted guardian of his ward Miss Rosa Bud, and as acting the part of general peacemaker in that turbulent tale of "Edwin Drood."

In "David Copperfield" there are several lawyers, but there is very little law. The nearest approach to a legal complication is the exposure of the humble Uriah Heep by Mr. Micawber, resulting in the recovery of Miss Betsy Trotwood's property, and the relief of the embarrassments of Mr. Wickfield, that genial and lovable specimen of the country solicitor, so very different from the Chancery lawyers of "Bleak House" or the sharp practitioners of "Pickwick." The weakness of old Mr. Wickfield, taken by itself, might seem contemptible, but in the hands of the master portrayer of character it is artistic, for Mr. Wickfield's facility was the necessary foil to Uriah Heep's roguery, just as the complications which resulted gave the opportunity to the unselfish and good-natured Tommy Traddles to right the wrongs of everybody all round. Mr. Traddles is probably the outcome of Dickens' own short attempt at keeping terms. He was in the life long enough to perceive the hard struggle which lies before the barrister without influence and connection ; and within his own circle Dickens, no doubt, knew many young barristers who went through the struggle of professional life of which Tommy Traddles was the impersonation.

Uriah Heep as a lawyer's clerk, and ultimately himself a legal practitioner, is entirely devoid of interest. As a man, his loyalty to his mother is, perhaps, the shadow of a redeeming feature in his character ; but as a lawyer he has no distinctive character at all, and from the legal side he illustrates nothing, unless it be that which is common to every phase of business life—that the

E

hypocrite is bound, sooner or later, to reveal himself, and that double-dealing usually recoils on the head of the cheat.

The other lawyers who figure in " David Copperfield" are Spenlow & Jorkins, the Doctor's Commons practitioners to whom David Copperfield became an articled clerk. But Mr. Spenlow is of interest rather as the father of Dora than as a lawyer, and his partner Mr. Jorkins is of interest only as illustrating a favourite device of Dickens, of playing off one partner of a legal firm against the other. Dodson played off his partner Fogg, Snitchey his partner Craggs, and Jorkins was the bogey of the firm of Spenlow & Jorkins. Says David Copperfield :

I was quite dismayed by the idea of this terrible Jorkins. But I found out afterwards that he was a mild man of a heavy temperament, whose place in the business was to keep himself in the background and be constantly exhibited by name as the most obdurate and ruthless of men. If a clerk wanted his salary raised, Mr. Jorkins wouldn't listen to such a proposition. If a client were slow to settle his bill of costs, Mr. Jorkins was resolved to have it paid, and however painful these things might be (and always were) to Mr. Spenlow's feelings, Mr. Jorkins would have his bond. The heart and hand of the good angel Spenlow would have been always open but for the restraining demon Jorkins.

To which description of Mr. Jorkins David quaintly adds :

As I have grown older, I think I have had experience of some other houses doing business on the principle of Spenlow & Jorkins.

The type of the provincial lawyer is exemplified by Mr. Wickfield and Uriah Heep in "David Copperfield," and by Snitchey & Craggs in "The Battle of Life." Wickfield and Heep of Canterbury had no humour. Snitchey and Craggs were full of the best kind of it, unconscious wit. When Dr. Jeddler the philosopher, whose theory was that nothing in life was serious, entertained Snitchy and Craggs at breakfast the morning the lawyers came to render an account of

their stewardship to Alfred Heathfield, the
doctor had quoted the French wit who had
expired with the remark, "The farce is ended;
draw the curtain."

"The French wit," said Mr. Snitchey, peeping sharply
into his blue bag, "was wrong, Dr. Jeddler, and your
philosophy is altogether wrong, depend upon it, as I
have often told you. *Nothing serious in life? What do
you call Law?*"

"A joke," replied the doctor.

"Did you ever go to law?" asked Mr. Snitchey.

"Never," returned the doctor.

"If you ever do," said Mr. Snitchey, "perhaps you'll
alter that opinion."

How intensely humorous also is Snitchey's
description of the landscape of an old battle-
field, which they looked at from Dr. Jeddler's
garden.

Here's a smiling country, once overrun by soldiers,
trespassers every man of them, and laid waste by fire and
sword.

Only a Dickens imagination could have
conceived of an invading army as "trespassers"! Then Snitchey goes on:

"But take this smiling country as it stands, think of the law appertaining to real property, to the bequest and device of real property, to the mortgage and redemption of real property, to leasehold, freehold, and copyhold estate. Think," said Mr. Snitchey, with such emotion that he actually smacked his lips, " of the complicated laws relating to title and proof of title, with all the contradictory precedents and numerous Acts of Parliament connected with them. Think of the infinite number of ingenious and interminable Chancery suits to which this pleasant prospect may give rise, and acknowledge, Dr. Jeddler, that there *is* a *green* spot in the scheme about us."

Almost every utterance of these two lawyers in "The Battle of Life" is humorous, and the story is full of legal sidelights, of which I shall mention only one, which to me has always seemed as full of humour as anything Dickens ever wrote. Two witnesses being required to Alfred's discharge to his trustees, Britain the serving man, and Clemency Newcombe the maid, were called. to sign as witnesses. Every lawyer who has had occasion to requisition the services of

country persons of no experience to witness
a deed knows how true to life is the description of the male and the female witness,
the seriousness of the one, the frivolity of
the other, and the deliberateness of both.

How Britain approached the deeds under protest, and
by dint of the doctor's coercion, and insisted on pausing
to look at them before writing, and also on turning them
round to see whether there was anything fraudulent
underneath, and how, having signed his name, he
became *desolate*, as one who had parted with his property
and rights, I want the time to tell, also how the blue
bag containing his signature afterwards had a mysterious
interest for him, and he couldn't leave it; also how
Clemency Newcombe, in an ecstasy of laughter at the
idea of her own importance and dignity, brooded over
the whole table with her two elbows, like a spread eagle,
and reposed her head upon her left arm, as a preliminary
to the formation of certain cabalistic characters, which
required a deal of ink, *and imaginary counterparts
whereof she executed at the same time with her tongue.*

The most unsavoury type of lawyer in all
Dickens' writings is Mr. Sampson Brass
in the "Old Curiosity Shop." He is a figure

only a degree less repulsive than his client
Mr. Daniel Quilp.

This Brass was an attorney of no very good repute,
from Bevis Marks in the City of London; he was a
tall, meagre man with a nose like a wen, and a protruding
forehead, retreating eyes, and hair of a deep red. He
wore a long black surtout reaching nearly to his ankles,
short black trousers, high shoes, and cotton stockings of
a bluish grey. He had a cringing manner, but a very
harsh voice; and his blandest smiles were so extremely
forbidding that, to have had his company under the
least repulsive circumstance, one would have wished him
to be out of temper that he might only scowl.

His first appearance is at the making of an
inventory of the contents of the Old Curiosity
Shop, when Quilp, the inexorable creditor,
entered upon possession. His last appearance
is when the law which he had outraged
overtook him in retribution, and the sentence
of the Court was :

That he should, for a term of years, reside in a spacious
mansion, where several other gentlemen were lodged
and boarded at the public charge, who went clad in a

sober uniform of grey turned up with yellow, had their hair cut extremely short, and chiefly lived on gruel and light soup.

The career of Mr. Sampson Brass is one continuous record of knavery. He is the only lawyer in the Dickens collection absolutely without any redeeming grace. He had not even a sense of humour, unless it be credited to him for humour that he employed his sister, Sally Brass, as "his clerk, assistant, housekeeper, secretary, confidential plotter, adviser, intriguer, and bill of costs increaser."

Sally Brass holds a unique place amongst the law clerks of Dickens, not merely because she is the only female law clerk, but also because she not only managed her brother's business, but managed her brother himself. The nearest approach to Miss Sally Brass amongst the numerous law clerks is Mr. Bazzard in " Edwin Drood," the confidential

clerk of Mr. Grewgious, of whom his master
rather stood in awe, much as Mr. Sampson
Brass stood in awe of his sister. Dickens'
description of Miss Brass once more
illustrates how there was ever present to
his mind a fixed hostility to the law and
all its ways :

In mind, she was of a strong and vigorous turn,
having from her earliest youth devoted herself with
uncommon ardour to the study of the law ; not wasting
her speculations upon its eagle flights, which are rare,
but tracing it attentively through all the slippery and
eel-like crawlings in which it commonly pursues its way.

The last word about Mr. Sampson Brass
is in the author's best satirical vein :

His name was erased and blotted out from the roll of
attorneys ; which erasure has been always held in these
latter times to be a great degradation and reproach, and
to imply the commission of some amazing villainy—as
indeed it would seem to be the case, when so many
worthless names remain among its better records,
unmolested.

One would like to think that Sampson Brass was an exception to the general rule that every Dickens lawyer is a type, and to regard Mr. Brass as an excrescence rather than as a natural feature in the legal profession ; but modern experience is too strong for this pleasing assumption. Since Dickens' day, and not least conspicuously within recent years, not a few lawyers have ended their careers in the dock ; and it is to be feared that the type is not yet extinct of the lawyer who, from greed of gain, lends his professional aid to the tortuous devices of an unscrupulous client, and ends by finding himself with too much time for reflection within prison walls.

Sampson Brass is the picture of one kind of professional failure in life. There is a different type of failure, and a much sadder one, in "A Tale of Two Cities," for Sydney Carton, in some respects the

most lovable character created by Dickens,
was a lawyer, although that fact is
apt to be forgotten, because the interest
which centres round him does not move on
the legal plane.   I speak of him, of course,
only in his legal aspect.   Whilst personally
he was the kind of man who would lay
down his life for his friend, I am afraid that
professionally he is also the type of man,
not unknown in the legal world, who
degrades his talents.   The only aspect in
which he is presented from the strictly
legal side is that of what is called
"devilling" to Mr. Stryver, the advocate
who defended Charles Darnay at the trial
for treason.

Mr. Stryver was a man of little more than thirty, but
looking twenty years older than he was, stout, loud, red,
bluff, and free from any drawback of delicacy.

It had once been noted at the bar that while Mr.
Stryver was a glib man, and an unscrupulous, and a
ready, and a bold, he had not that faculty of extracting

the essence from a heap of statements which is among the most striking and necessary of the advocate's accomplishments. But a remarkable improvement came upon him as to this. The more business he got, the greater his power seemed to grow of getting at its pith and marrow, and however late at night he sat carousing with Sydney Carton, he always had his points at his finger ends in the morning.

The explanation was simple. Sydney Carton was supplying the brains, and Stryver was getting the success. It is a sad picture that of the jackal and the lion carousing together whilst Carton did the "boiling down" of the busy advocate's papers, which on the morrow Stryver should use to further his success, whilst poor Carton's work was unrecognised. Unutterably sad is the reflection of this clever, but lost, lawyer as he walked home in the early morning after a carousal with Stryver :

Waste forces within him, and a desert all around, this man stood still on his way across a silent terrace and saw for a moment lying in the wilderness before him a mirage

of honourable ambition, self-denial, and perseverance;
sadly, sadly the sun rose; it was upon no sadder sight
than the man of good abilities and good emotions,
incapable of their directed exercise, incapable of his own
help and his own happiness, sensible of the blight on him
and resigning himself to let it eat him away.

I am afraid that in the law, as in other
walks of . life, there are many failures, of
whom Sydney Carton is a type.

I have barely tapped the legal mine of
interest in Dickens. I have but glanced at
some of the more outstanding aspects of the
subject, and the more outstanding personali-
ties. There are other aspects, and other
individuals, over whom one would like to
linger and to speculate. Delightful possi-
bilities seem to lurk in many of the minor
legal characters, such as Mr. Phunky, the
bashful junior counsel for Pickwick, or the
roisterous Lowton, Mr. Perker's clerk, and
the law clerks who held high revel under his
presidency at The Magpie and Stump, or

the meek-mannered Jackson, the clerk of
Dodson & Fogg. But to exhaust the legal
interest in the works of Charles Dickens
would want a bulky volume.

Some of the Dickens lawyers are eccentric
and some commonplace ; some are dry-as-
dust, some very human ; no two of them are
alike, and each is typical of a class to be
found in the legal profession in the present
day, just as in the time of Dickens. That,
by his writings, Dickens drew public attention
to some of the cruel features of the law as it
existed in his day, especially as regards
imprisonment for debt, and that his writings
were a powerful factor in removing or soften-
ing hard features of the judicial system, there
is no doubt. But there are anomalies and
evils denounced in his books still unremedied.
There is yet a wide field open to the Dickens
student, in the judicial aspect of Dickens'
works, and my aim has been accomplished if

I have been able, in some degree, to flash a little light upon this undeveloped mine of interest, and in some small measure to create, as regards the attitude of Charles Dickens to the law, a desire on the part of others to inquire further into a subject so teeming with interest.

www.ingramcontent.com/pod-product-compliance
Lightning Source LLC
Chambersburg PA
CBHW030509100426
42813CB00002B/407